UNITED STATES SENATE
WASHINGTON, D.C.

DANIEL K. INOUYE
HAWAII

July 25, 2012

Dear Mr. Chun:

Thank you for sharing with me a copy of your book, <u>The C.Q. Yee Hop Story: In Memory of An "American Dream"</u>. Your thoughtfulness is deeply appreciated.

Aloha,

DANIEL K. INOUYE
United States Senator

Mr. Junion Klai Chun
1019 Hourglass Place
Diamond Bar, California 91765

A Chinese Immigrant's
Success Story 1867-1954

C. Q. Yee Hop
Achieves his American Dream

Copyright © 2015 by Junion Klai Chun

All Rights Reserved.

Translation from Chinese by William D. Won, September, 1988

Edited by Clara C. Won, September, 1988

Prepared and summarized by Junion Klai Chun, September, 2011

Revised by Junion Klai Chun, March, 2015

ISBN-13: 978-1508945307

ISBN-10: 1508945306

Contents

Dedication..2

Forward..4

Introduction..14

Autobiography (1947)

Chapter 1 (Ancestral Background)..........................18

Chapter 2 (Immigration: From China With Love)...28

Chapter 3 (Entrepreneurships)..................................36

Chapter 4 (Who's who – 3 Family Generations).........98

Commentary..108

Miscellaneous (Congratulatory messages, poems in Chinese, etc)..116

Corporate Headquarters: C.Q. Yee Hop Plaza
Honolulu, Hawaii

* C.Q. Yee Hop Co., Ltd.
* Yee Hop Ltd. (Ranch)
* Yee Hop Realty Ltd.
* American Brewing Co., Ltd.
* Hawaiian Hardwood Co., Ltd.
* Yee Hop & Sons Ltd.

DEDICATION

I dedicate this book, "A CHINESE IMMIGRANT'S SUCCESS STORY (1867 – 1954) in fond memory of my late grandfather, C.Q. Yee Hop and to my numerous uncles, aunts, and cousins.

His business achievement brought peace and prosperity to our family and provided a strong American lifestyle full of hope and inspiration to future generations.

****

Part of C.Q. Yee Hop's
81st Birthday gifts.

FOREWARD

"If you want to learn about money, learn from someone who has a lot of it."

Charles J. Givens

Following my retirement in 1995, I have been studying many best selling financial self-help books. It became an obsession with me to learn more about proven strategies for accumulating wealth through smart investments.

Since I am blessed with some savings and a small inheritance, I honestly thought that with my extensive business and academic experience, building a personal fortune and living the good life in retirement would be a "piece of cake". ....However, my expectation did not pan out as easily as I expected.

According to Robert T. Kiyosaki ("Rich Dad, Poor Dad"): "The main reason people struggle financially is because they spent years in school but learned nothing about money. The result is, <u>people learn to work for money.....but never</u>

learn to have money work for them." (As an adjunct community college business instructor, I find this to be a worthy lesson to follow.)

Nevertheless, even if such financial skills are not taught in most schools, many rich and famous people have become enormously successful even with little or no formal education.

Such a person was my late grandfather, C.Q. Yee Hop (C.Q. or Chun Quon was his Chinese name; Yee Hop was the store name of a small meat market in Honolulu). In 1886, at age 19, in spite of the discriminatory CHINESE ECLUSION ACT (C.E.A., 1882), he emigrated from China to America in search of the "American Dream".

This decision must have taken a lot of courage since the C.E.A. restricted Chinese immigration to the United States. It was enacted in response to economic fears where native born Americans attributed unemployment and declining wages to Chinese workers whom they viewed as racially inferior. In addition this law prohibited Chinese from becoming U.S. Citizens.

We may never know what really prompted my late grandfather to take such risks. However, we do know despite having to face decades of adversities, he still was able to lift himself out of the poverty to become one of Hawaii's early business leaders.

As a highlight in 1947 during the celebration of C.Q. Yee Hop's 81st birthday, he was very happy to look back over his life that was full not only of business accomplishments and material wealth, but also rich in family and friends.

From the president of China, from prominent American government officials and many friends came personal scripts, poems, congratulatory messages and wonderful gifts.

Traditionally, as the oldest grandson (on the male side of the family), I feel a filial obligation to put together and re-introduce my grandfather's 1947 autobiography entitled "TRIBUTE TO MR. C.Q.

YEE HOP ON HIS 81ST BIRTHDAY" as a sentimental memorial.

The memoir you are reading is a story told in his own word.

It is my fondest hope that due to C.Q. Yee Hop's past endeavors to his community and to his country, this autobiography about a successful entrepreneur might inspire and encourage other potential hopefuls to also "go for broke" and capture the "American Dream".

Finally, I am truly grateful for the translation from Chinese to English by William D. Won and edited by Clara C. Won. It was mainly through their remarkable contributions that helped to make this renewed autobiography possible.

Junion Klai Chun

March, 2015

Map of China

*Gong Bui Village,
  Heong Shan County,
    Guangdong Province

INTRODUCTION

1947

In following a popular Chinese custom, my sixteen children and zealous grandchildren are honoring me on my 81st birthday in Honolulu.

For this celebration, countless friends from here and abroad have favored me with lavishly laudatory poetry, congratulatory messages, and tributes filled with generous good wishes and overwhelming high praises. Friends and colleagues of the New Chinese

Daily News in Honolulu, together with those of C.Q. Yee Hop and Company Ltd., and the American Brewing Co., Ltd., were kind enough to have the festivities of this occasion compiled and recorded in print and pictures in a commemorative booklet.

In retrospect, I was urged to put down in writing my recollections of events and experiences of the past eighty years so that my children and grandchildren will have an account and understanding of the hardships, difficulties, adversities, and failures, as well as the successes of my life-long career in establishing several lucrative businesses in Hawaii.

By all means this autobiography is not intended for self-glorification. Rather, if anything, it is more of a self-gratification.

Nov. 11, 1947

C.Q. Yee Hop

The Chun's Family Ancestral Shrine
Honolulu, Hawaii
Left: C.Q. Yee Hop & his younger brothers
Chun Young and Chun Chin
(paying homeage to their mother)

Autobiography

Chapter 1

Ancestral Background

During my lifetime, I was never an official, never a hero, never a tycoon, never an inventor. Therefore, there is nothing really noteworthy to boast about except to serve as a role model or example for younger generations. On the other hand, I believe that, while I am still capable of doing it, the eighty-one years of my experience (with their successes, failures, and hardships) should be recorded. This may be of benefit and value as a reference.

I was born in the sixth year of the T'ung Chih (1862-74) reign of the Ch'ing Dynasty (1644-1911) on the nineteenth day of the eighth month according to the lunar calendar in 1867 in GuangDong Province, GongBui Village, to a Chun family. My father was Chun Yau Jun. Following in his father's footsteps and those of my forefathers, he made a livelihood in farming. These were peaceful and prosperous times, so he earned an adequate living. Together with my mother, whose maiden surname was Chong, they provided us children with a simple but happy and contented family life.

While I was growing up, I often listened raptly to the village elders as they recounted tales of the Chun clan's origin in the area. In China's long history there have occurred three great migrations from the North; migrations to escape invading barbarians from across the northern borders, famine, oppression, despotism or tyranny and to seek a better life in a more favorable climate and environment.

With Forefather Mun Loong Kung, the clan migrated southward eventually ending up in Chungshan County in GuangDong Province during the Sung Dynasty (960-1219). He established the first generation there. One generation later, Forefather Tien Gork Kung was commemorated for his contributions to the building of the county's capital city. In 1278, Kublai Khan's army entered China. Emperor Wei Huang, during his escape, passed through our area Tien Gork Kung led a reception to welcome him. The Emperor stayed three nights and then moved on. In

1279, Kublai Khan completed his conquest and became Emperor of China. So began the Yuan Dynasty (1279-1368). For their earlier association and collaboration with the Sung regime, all those with the Chun surname were sought out and targeted for persecution. For generations during the Yuan Dynasty, no Chun dared to disclose his identity. Not until about the seventeenth generation did the Chuns feel safe enough to reclaim and resume their true surname.

The Chuns who settled in Chungshan were mostly farmers. My grandfather, Chun Sung Dee was one the most prosperous. He owned many tens of "mou" (.60 acre equals 1 mou) of farmland. Harvests were more than sufficient to support his family. After my father inherited the properties, he added poultry husbandry to his farming activities by raising geese. Thus, the twenty-fourth generation, to which my brothers and I belong, was exposed and fated to become farmers and/or agriculturists.

I have two younger brothers, Chun Young and Chun Chin. Both are residing in Honolulu with their families. I have three older sisters. One is married to a Chang, the other two each married a Lee. I also have three younger sisters, who married a Chong, a Pang and a Chee. Only my younger sister who married Pang lives in Honolulu. Each of them enjoys a houseful of children and grandchildren. My businesses have provided employment to many of their sons who have come to Hawaii to earn money to support their families back in China.

OFFICE OF THE MAYOR
HONOLULU

JOHN H. WILSON

June 22, 1947

To the Honorable

CHUN QUON YEE HOP

Greetings and Felicitations

On this glorious and joyous occasion when breaks the roseate dawn on the Ninth Decade in your blessed and fruitful life, may we of the City and County of Honolulu join with your myriads of friends in offering to you our heartfelt congratulations and our most ardent wishes that health and prosperity may continue to walk with you through many more years and may you be blessed with a hundred sons and a thousand grandsons.

John H. Wilson, Mayor

John M. Asing, Supervisor
Manuel C. Pacheco, Supervisor
Milton D. Beamer, Supervisor
Richard M. Kageyama, Supervisor
Noble K. Kauhane, Supervisor
Nicholas T. Teves, Supervisor
Ben F. Dillingham, Supervisor
Leonard K. Fong, Auditor
Wm. Chung-Hoon, Jr., Treasurer
Leon K. Sterling, Sr., Clerk
Duke P. Kahanamoku, Sheriff

Office Of The Mayor
Honolulu
1947

欲行千里始於足下

"The Journey of a Thousand Mile Begins With a Single Step."

Chinese Proverb

Chapter 2

Immigration: From China With Love

My childhood education was quite limited. I did not enroll in school until the age of nine to study the old classics. At age fourteen, I had to abandon schooling to help in my father's firewood business located in a local marketplace, Sah Kai Hee which served the nearby hamlets and villages. My responsibilities included chopping wood and cooking for several employees. It was laboriously hard work, but

I was happy and enjoyed working for my father.

When I was eighteen years old, a cousin, Chun Pun Lin, had just returned from America where he had gone to live with a brother, Chun Kum Moon in "Old Golden Mountain (San Francisco), California and in the "Sandalwood Mountains" (Honolulu), Hawaiian Island. He regaled me with fascinating stories of those places. I was particularly impressed with his descriptions of the rapid economic growth and diverse opportunities available overseas.

His accounts stirred within me a great desire to go there to make my living. This desire eventually inspired me to formulate plans to travel to the Hawaiian Islands to seek my fortune. My old father understood my ambition and cheerfully encouraged me to carry on.

The following year, 1886, I was nineteen years old. My father and I journeyed to Hong Kong. He helped me obtain the proper papers for going overseas and then made all the necessary preparations for passage to America. I sailed away on the steamship S.S. New York

City after bidding my father goodbye. I could not help feeling a deep sadness as I departed.

Crossing the Pacific Ocean took twenty seven days before we docked in San Francisco. At that time, there was no direct sailing nor docking from the Far East to Hawaii.

When I stepped ashore in San Francisco, I mentally compared my situation with that Columbus when he first viewed the Americas. For a long time I stood still to survey the horizon; first to the right and then to the left of me. I was in a totally different new world! However, when my thoughts suddenly turned to my old parents so far away at home, I could not refrain from being tense and emotional and terribly homesick.

Here in a new land I had no plans for a livelihood. Arriving in San Francisco, I had ninety cents Hong Kong money remaining in my pocket and that was only twenty five cents in American money! I looked up a kinsman from my village, Chun Tim, who farmed a fruit ranch in Suisun Valley, about forty miles northeast from San Francisco. I travelled there to seek temporary employment and lodging.

I worked in the orchards for about three weeks; then I found passage on a ship to the Hawaiian Islands, my original destination. Upon landing in Honolulu, I was soon able to find a job in a butcher shop near the waterfront. As I toiled, I realized that this was akin to my earlier experiences working in my father's village firewood store. Thus I decided to devote my efforts toward learning all I could about this area of business, the buying and selling of merchandise.

Old C.Q. Yee Hop Market
Chinatown, 1940

Chapter 3

Entrepreneurship: Trials and Tribulation

C.Q. Yee Hop & Co., Ltd.

The following year, 1887, I opened the Yee Hop Meat Market in Honolulu on Maunakea Street. However, inadequate capital produced insufferable crises one after another. Despite extreme hardships and difficulties, I struggled along with forbearance, fortitude, and perseverance. Nevertheless, I enjoyed the independence. The market managed to survive for over a year. Then a friend, Lum Hop, joined me in the venture. Together we formed a congenial partnership and labored diligently for success. This business partnership lasted for over twelve years.

Throughout this period the Hawaiian Islands was a monarchy. King Kalakaua (1874 – 1891) was on the throne. As with our little business struggling to survive, it was also a critical period in the history of the Islands. In 1887, Kalakaua was compelled to promulgate a new constitution. An armed insurrection by his opposition took place in 1989.

Queen Liliuokulani, who succeeded Kalakaua, was deposed in 1893. Annexation of Hawaii by the United Stated was accepted by a joint resolution of the U.S. Congress in 1898 and the Territory of Hawaii was established on 14 June 1900.

Engrossed as I was in my efforts to establish a foothold in the business world, I was but a mute witness to these historic events. Moreover, I had married and was starting a family during this time. In two more years, I was also to lose the mother of my four children.

Most of our customers spoke Hawaiian. Before long, through necessity and practice, I, too, was able to speak fluent Hawaiian. It was important for business. However, with annexation to the United States, English became the language of the land. I had a limited knowledge of and almost no ability to speak or read it. It was then I decided I should take lessons. An American lady who lived in Pauoa Valley gave evening English lessons to people like me. Each evening after closing the market, I lit my way to her house with a kerosene lantern held in one hand to attend the lessons. After the long hours and hard work at the market each day it became increasingly difficult for me to keep up this nightly routine. Moreover, money for tuition could not be spared. In three weeks, reluctantly, I was forced to discontinue. Thus ended another aspect of my brief and meager educational pursuits.

In 1900, bubonic plague broke out in Honolulu. It threatened to reach epidemic proportions. The authorities ordered certain sections of the city set afire to eliminate the rats whose fleas carried the plague disease. A quarantine isolated those areas. Unfortunately, a shift in the winds caused the fires to rage uncontrolled, and the downtown area including Chinatown went up in flames! At the time, I was outside the quarantine zone. I stood helplessly beside the barricades erected to keep the citizens away and watched with alarm, fear, and dismay as our market burned to the ground. It was a disaster, we lost everything.

Long after the ashes had cooled and the area was cleaned, the task of rebuilding began in 1902. Altogether we had devoted thirteen long years of hard work to our business, and we were reluctant to abandon our hopes for success in the promising economic growth and future of Hawaii. We formed a new Yee Hop Company, set our capitalization at $8,000 with me and seven other shareholders each putting up $1,000 apiece, Most of us were butchers or would-be butchers:

Lum Hop

Lum Tung

Lum Heen

Lee Bew (my nephew)

Chun Sun

Chun Young (my brother)

Chun Chin (my brother)

Our store on Maunakea Street soon became too cramped for our expanding business. We needed a larger store, so the market was moved to Alakea Street.

In order to distinguish ourselves from a smaller store that happened to have the same name, Yee Hop, we decided to add my initials C(hun) Q(uon) in English to the company name. Thus it became known as C.Q. Yee Hop and Company. For five years, the business prospered and grew steadily. Again we had to find larger quarters. Subsequently, we relocated to our present King Street location.

By 1912, each $1,000 share of stock had grown in value to $4,000. All together, our original investment now totaled $32,000.

We raised our capitalization another $8,000 by issuing eight new shares at $1,000 each to the follow eight shareholders:

    Wong Heen

    Pang Sing Choy
    (my brother-in-law)

    Chun Sing

    Chong Kam Cheong

    Lum Mew Ching

    Yuen Chin Sung

    Lau Wun

    Young Sing Kee
    (Samuel K. Young)

Profit and cash-flow had increased to such an extent that the company was incorporated in 1920 and became C.Q. Yee Hop and Co., Ltd. Our stock values grew to $200,000; by 1925 to $250,000; by 1927 to $300,000; by 1930 to $500,000. All this came about because of excellent profitability. There was never a request made to our stockholders to put in additional cash for operational uses.

From 1930 on, I was becoming more and more preoccupied with other enterprises, so that less of my attention was being directed to the running of C.Q. Yee Hop and Company. Consequently, for the decade that followed, while business was good and solid, annual earnings were down.

World War II exploded in our midst in 1941. Thousands of troops were stationed here and many more thousands came through on their way to and from the Pacific war zones. All types of business and industries flourished and enjoyed the boom. Merchants, large and small, were inevitably prospering under this wartime economy. For C.Q. Yee Hop and Co., however, both the business and earning were not remarkable. This caused me deep concern and a great deal of thoughtful contemplations and lots of sleepless nights.

When, in 1945, stockholder and general manager, Samuel K. Young, suddenly proposed a takeover by buying me out. I was naturally surprised, stunned, and shocked by this move. That was certainly an astonishing and emotional encounter. For me to consider giving up my lifelong accomplishment and everything that I had achieved with hard work and sweat, and to cut off my association with the company, was entirely out of the question!

Instead, I countered by proposing to buy him out at a very high price for his shares and those in his group. As a result, Mr. Young resigned his managership in November 1945. Following in his footsteps twelve key men, department heads and other personnel resigned.

I was thankful that, despite my seventy eight years, I was still physically fit, healthy, and mentally alert. I immediately assumed leadership in running the business with the help of my four sons. By year end, our company had accumulated more than $800,000 in capital.

Where it is located at King and Maunakea streets, the company was its own landlord as well as the owner of a large scale icehouse. Twenty-two delivery trucks made daily deliveries of meat and groceries all over the city and the island of Oahu. With 115 employees, the monthly payroll was over $50,000. This concept of business was what I had established so many years ago. However, due to the lack of resourceful personnel and adequate human capacity, the progress that could have been attained after sixty years of effort was not impressive compared to other enterprises. I regret that it is so.

From a small, one-man meat stall in 1887, Yee Hop Market grew and developed into a multi-department, multi-service "super" market by the 1920-30s doing both retail and wholesale business in meats and groceries. We served the general public, other stores and markets, restaurants, public institutions, and schools, steamships, and round-the-world cruise liners that came and went through the port of Honolulu, as well as military transports, warships, commissaries, and post exchanges. Self-sufficiency provided the basis for growth whenever and wherever it was need.

The meat market employed about ten full-time butchers who cut meats to order and sold over the counter. We featured meats, bacon, hot dog, butter, etc. packed under our own brand name of "PARADISE". A pork department sold fresh island pork. We specialized in Chinese style cut-up roast pork and barbecued pork (cha-siu) and roast whole suckling pigs prepared in a specially built

Chinese high-heat oven. To support the department, a slaughterhouse in Kalihi was built to dress and prepare the hogs for our own use and for that of other stores. I used to get up at three a.m. to drive by horse cart down the Pali in the dark with Sam Kam, a young employee, to scour the small farms in the area to buy hogs for slaughter and sale. Later we built several pens to raise hogs and pigs. On the same tract of land in Kalihi, a truck farm also flourished where Chinese and western vegetables of all kinds were grown the way it was done in so many villages in Southern China, tended by employees newly arrived from China with experience in farming.

The produce department in the market regularly brought in choice seasonal fruits and vegetable from the mainland, and the grocery department's shelves were stocked with only the best brands of canned goods and staples such as S&W, Prince, Libby, and Del Monte.

We hired a master baker to set up a full-scale bakery on the second floor above the market. Every day the bakery produced fresh breads and all varieties of cookies and cakes, the most popular and best-known being strawberry shortcake with luscious, fresh strawberries and real whipped cream. All products from the bakery were sold exclusively downstairs in the market.

Housewives throughout the city, who wanted to do their grocery shopping by telephone, called in their daily orders, which were then gathered and delivered to their kitchens that morning or afternoon by a fleet of four or five light Ford trucks-to the Nuuanu, Manoa, Kaimuki, Waikiki, or Kalihi districts of Honolulu. Several heavy trucks made regular deliveries to our commercial customers.

Since our meat products were brought into Honolulu wholly by ships or freighters, five to seven days en route from the Mainland in a frozen or chilled state, it became necessary that we have adequate storage. Thus, in 1927 a full-scale icehouse was built in the warehouse area behind the main store. This three story building also housed a dormitory on the second floor. The third floor was rented to a German we called "Baron" who operated a gymnasium. I spent many hours exercising there.

The dormitory was home to twenty or more single men employees, most of whom had families in their native villages in China. As an adjunct to the dormitory, we operated a dining room for the convenience of our employees. A full-time crew of three cooked and served rice and three or four Chinese dishes at each meal, with a more elaborate and extensive Sunday dinner. There were at least forty or more people eating there regularly.

In addition to C.Q. Yee Hop and Company, I also found the King Market in 1907, located next door to Yee Hop. Stalls and store spaces were rented out to a variety of businesses. I assumed the position of treasurer to oversee and manage its financial affairs. From the very beginning it was a profitable enterprise. At one time, for each share of stock at $25 par, we were able to pay a dividend of $1.00 per month. This represented a record-breaking dividend payment in any business in the Islands, if not the nation. The King Market was consistently a profit-making venture. It was regrettable, however, that no all-out efforts were made to have it developed and expanded into a larger and more varied facility.

Kona, Hawaii Ranch, 25,000 acres

As I have stated earlier, my interest and inclination have been toward agriculture and animal husbandry. Therefore, I was always hopeful that C.Q. Yee Hop and Company Ltd., will ultimately be able to raise and supply its own meat products, particularly island beef. So, when the opportunity presented itself, we located and purchased 25,000 acres of land on the slopes of island of Hawaii's Mauna Loa in southwest Kona to add to the company assets and to fulfill my hope. Again, sadly, due to preoccupation with other projects and the separation of distance between islands, I was not able to devote full attention to its development. Consequently, meat production was very meager and able only to supply a fraction of what the meat market required. Nevertheless, in the efforts that were expended, we managed build up, at the maximum, a herd of about 750 cattle.

I frequently travelled to Kona to ride horseback all day alongside our paniolos (Hawaiian cowboys) to check on the cattle, drive them from one grazing area to another, or to round them up for shipment to Honolulu.

Inter Island Steamship Company, who provided the only available transportation between the islands, did not maintain a regular shipping schedule to and from the Kona Coast, only to Hilo. Only upon request and upon shipping demands did they dispatch their ships to deliver or pick up freight at landings at Hookena, Miloli (closest to our ranch) and at Kailua. Sometimes the cattle were herded down the mountain to the landings, driven into the shallow water so they could wade out to the waiting ship and be hauled aboard.

The ranch property encompasses an area from the beach at sea level, past the "government road" (around the island highway) up the slopes of Mauna Loa to an elevation of about 7000 feet. It is land interspersed with lava flows from the dormant caldera on top of the mountain. It is land dense and overgrown with lush tropical growth of vines, poha berries, giant tree ferns, ohia and koa trees. It is land that is home to wild boars, pheasants and numerous species of tropical birds. There are also cleared area where cattle can graze.

To our amazement and delight, we discovered stands of large Koa and Ohia trees scattered throughout the mountainous area at the 4,000 feet elevation. Nurtured by the warm sun and cool fog, these trees flourished and grew and became a treasured wood suitable for the fine furniture and other uses. Acacia Koa is a large hardwood timber tree endemic to the

Hawaiian Islands. It can grow straight up to a height of forty feet and maybe six to eight feet around at the bottom. The Ohia is a smaller tree with bright red flowers and a very hard dense wood found to be most suitable for flooring. So, in 1920, we established a Koawood Division within C.Q. Yee Hop and Company and called it the Hawaiian Mahogany Company.

In order to develop its commercial potential, in 1921, I bought the forfeited Bolte Brothers Sawmill in Kona, located adjacent to our land. It included 1,198 acres of land and two sawmills, "lumbering equipment, machinery and all tools, implements and all the trees felled and severed from aforesaid and all timber manufactured therefrom", as specified in the sales agreement. Occasionally, I relived my joyous boyhood experience by serving as a woodcutter there.

I sent to Kona Yee Chee, a loyal young employee at the market, to oversee the land and the operation. The trees were felled with two-men, ten-foot-long crosscut saw and hauled or dragged by caterpillar tractor through the undergrowth and forest to the two sawmills located four miles apart:

the higher band saw mill cut only koa, the other mill used a large circular saw for ohia, which grew at lower elevations. The whole operation was done under extremely crude, exhausting, and difficult conditions. Still we were able to produce the lumber dictated by orders from Honolulu. It was hauled down to different village landings along the Kona Coast to await shipment to the Honolulu lumberyard where it was stacked, cured, and sold. We became one of the major suppliers of koa and ohia wood in the islands.

Hawaiian Hardwood Company, Ltd.

In Honolulu a woodwork and cabinet shop was also put into operation to manufacture koa wood furniture of bedroom sets, dining room tables and chairs, cabinets, shelves as well as curios such as calabashes, ukuleles, pictures frames, vases, and lamp bases. It also did millwork of all kinds with two brothers, experienced carpenters and cabinet makers from China, named Lau Chut and Lau Bat, who designed and copied koa furniture to order.

Many of these products are in use today in scores of households throughout the islands. In recent years, when monkey pod wood products became so popular, we set up a small production line operation to design and manufacture carved leaf trays, salad bowls and utensils, turned wood serving dishes and bowls, perfume bottle holders and other decorative objects. Altogether an investment of $280,000 was spent for this development.

In 1939, the Koa wood division was separated from the parent company and reorganized as an independent operation and renamed Hawaiian Hardwood Company. It was barely profitable.

When World War II broke out, the Hawaiian Hardwood Company contracted to supply the United States Navy with all the ohia lumber it needed to keel blocks and lumber for ship rebuilding and ship repairs and for its dry docks. Despite manpower and material shortages, we also continued, on a smaller scale, to manufacture decorative wooden products to boost hometown morale and for economic purposes as part of the war effort.

My love for the ranch and my lifelong belief in its great potentials have always been strong, steadfast, and firm. In my private thinking, ranching can be developed into a highly profitable enterprise here. But, because of my advancing age and diminishing vitality, "my energy does not follow my heart's dictates". I cannot attain the goal of further developments. This affects me deeply and sorrowfully.

Now that I have reached eighty-one years of age, there are one or two more matters I should mention briefly. In 1932, while on a trip to China, reports were transmitted to me that the United States Congress was about to repeal the Prohibition Act, the Eighteenth Amendment, which had kept the country dry for so many years. During that time, no alcohol products were allowed to be manufactured or sold in the country. There was bootlegging, of course, along with speakeasies and serious crime.

AMERICAN BREWING CO., LTD.
Honolulu, Hawaii

American Brewing Co., Ltd. ("Royal Beer")

Upon my return to Honolulu in the beginning of 1933, C.Q. Yee Hop and Company and I joined in an equal partnership with a capital of $200,000 to form a brewing company to produce beer. The repeal of Prohibition took effect in March 1933. In the meantime, with my eldest son, Yee Sing, I personally made a shopping trip to the Mainland seeking a brew master and buying equipment such as a large copper brew kettle, wooden and glass-lined steel tanks for fermenting and aging, bottling machinery, and other necessary equipment.

Originally when Prohibition first went into effect in 1919, an old brewery at 547 South Queen Street was shut down and the property sold. It consisted of the land plus a tall, multi-story, red brick building, the brew house, a wood frame office building, an engine room, garages, and many storage buildings, and an artesian well. I bought the property as a speculative investment.

In May 1933, the American Brewing Company, Ltd., was formed. The old brewery was reclaimed, rebuilt, restored, and remodeled, made ready to produce beer again. Thomas Eaton, an Englishman from Montara, California, was hired as brew master. "Ambrew" became our brand name. We had high hopes that Eaton could produce a good product. Unfortunately, his beer did not appeal to the taste buds of the local people; perhaps it was more suitable for an Englishman's taste. As a result, the beer did not sell well. This was definitely a setback. It was a very bitter disappointment.

Again, because of demands of my businesses, I did not pay attention to the facts. Refusing to be disheartened, the company struggled to survive for the next six years during which time the brewery underwent a reorganization, two changes of management, two change of brew masters, and eight changes of managers. We lost $300,000 to $400,000. I, myself, suffered a loss of approximately $400,000.

There were recurring problems with our workers who had become unionized as part of the ILWU. At various times we had strikes and threats of strikes over union demands. Oahu Ice and Cold Storage Company started up a brewery, and Primo Beer entered the small Hawaiian market. We also had to compete for business with imported mainland beers such as Acme, Rainier, Schlitz, Miller High Life, and Lucky Lager. Business was very bad.

Friends advised me to give up the brewery in order not to affect the other enterprises. After probing why others could succeed where I had failed, I determined to concentrate on recouping the brewery business. In 1939, I bought up all the other shares and ran the business myself and reduced the losses to a certain extent. Finally, armed with faith and dogged determination to fulfill my hopes and expectation, I solicited and regained control of the business. I stepped in to serve as its chief executive officer and manager. As part of the changes, the beer now became known as Royal Beer and bore the Hawaiian coat of arms on its label.

It was very gratifying, indeed, to be able to see a steady improvement in both the sales and the financial picture; particularly during the World War II period when there was an explosive demand for beer. From these earnings, we were able to recover all our previous losses. It was a blessing.

Yee Hop Realty Ltd.

As of last year (1946), I had all our real estate-related enterprises consolidated to form Yee Hop Realty Company, as a means to facilitate management and expansion. In terms of the latter, we successfully negotiated to be appointed Honolulu representatives and brokers for the Central Insurance Company, the United Insurance Company and the Pacific Insurance Company. Each year the basic needs of insurance coverages of all kinds for all of our enterprises are quite extensive. Not only are we now able to provide this service for ourselves, we can also do it for our friends and clientele. Earlier this year, as an added convenience, we ventured into another area of service; namely, a safe deposit box rental business. Box installation is near completion at 115 North King Street.

In retrospect, in the course of my sixty-one years of efforts in the business world, I have always enjoyed the challenge and appreciated the cooperation and support of my friends, colleagues, and loyal employees: while there were inevitable ups and downs along the way, I consider myself very fortunate, indeed, that I had never suffered great nor irreparable financial losses, for, after all, I landed on American soil with only ninety cents HK in my pocket. For my business, I am grateful for the courtesy, kindness and goodwill the people of Hawaii have shown me. These, and good fortune, as well, constitute some of the significant factors that enabled me to build what our business enterprises are today. As a matter of record, it is a source of personal pride for me to report the assets of each company here.

C.Q. Yee Hop and Company, Ltd.
$500,000.00

Yee Hop Realty, Ltd.
$300,000.00

American Brewing Co., Ltd.
$250,000.00

Yee Hop, Ltd. (ranch)
$300,000.00

Yee Hop and Sons
$200,000.00

There are other small businesses I have not included. Of all my life's labors, these are the fruits.

Chinese Constitutional Conference, Nanking, China 1946

Chinese Constitutional Party, a failed reality

Even though my life and my time have been devoted to commerce, there were times when the feeling came that I might not have contributed my share to my country and to society. During my early years the political situation in China was precarious. Under this unstable situation, there appeared two brilliant patriotic scholars, Kang Yau Wei and Liang Kai Chiao. Together they championed and worked toward establishing a constitutional government to replace the existing corrupt, despotic regime without using force. However farfetched this seemed to be, they won my respect and admiration just the same. In 1990, Mr. Liang came to Honolulu to appeal for political and financial support in order to carry out his mission. When he took steps to form a chapter of his fledgling Constitutional Party here, I and many compatriots became members. However, the 1911 revolution led by Dr. Sun Yat Sen overthrew the imperial Ching government, and the Constitutional Party thus became defunct and inactive. Then, unexpectedly, just two years ago, in 1945, the Party was revived in China and the surviving members (I among them) were invited to go to Nanking, to take part in a national assembly of all political parties for joint discussion on the formulation and adoption of a new constitution. I met President Chiang Kai Shek and other well-known officials. I felt proud, honored, and so humble. Before long, however, the power struggle between the Kuomingtang and the Communist Party broke out into a long drawn-out war. Thus, history was repeating itself; the concept of constitutional government was again not to become a reality.

Mun Lun Chinese Language School

Although I was a participant in this so-called local "political activism", I had never really entertained any thoughts nor sought any political roles here or abroad. On the other hand, community services here were more of my concern. So, about thirty years ago, I organized a group of people to found the Mun Lun Chinese Language School in Honolulu. At one time, the peak enrollment was over 1,400 students. Soon, the school distinguished itself, not only academically, but as the largest institution of its kind in existence in the United States.

In 1929, I owned the leases on properties adjacent to Mun Lun School. I persuaded Bishop Trust, the owner of this land, to sell several lots to the school so that it might gain direct access to the public street. Not only did I make a large donation myself, I also spearheaded the drive to raise the necessary funds to meet the purchase price. Through subscriptions and donations from the community and shows put on by students, the drive was a huge success. Not only did Mun Lun

School gain a wide entryway, there was sufficient land for the construction of a new and much-needed multi-classroom building.

With other village kinsmen living here in Honolulu, I helped raise money to finance the building of a large school in our native village of Gong Bui. They named the school "The Chun Quon School" after me.

Chinese Chamber of Commerce

Recognizing the need and advantages of an organization to represent our interests here in Honolulu, twelve young Chinese businessmen and I founded in 1911 the Chinese Merchants Association, the forerunner of today's Chinese Chamber of Commerce of Hawaii. I offered the use of the second floor of the Yee Hop Market to the group rent free. This became the headquarters of the Chamber for over two years until enough money was raised for it to put up its own building on Maunakea Street. The Chamber became one of the leading civic and commercial organizations in the Honolulu community. Declining all requests to serve in any official capacity because of the demands of my businesses, I nevertheless was very active in its many community affairs and money-raising drives for its many causes, such as flood relief in China and local disasters.

Publishing: New China Daily (Honolulu); Chinese World (San Francisco); Humanity Weekly (Hong Kong)

In the recent decade, I financed the operation of the New China Daily in Honolulu which was the beginning and growth of Chinese presses in the islands. Likewise, I also gave financial support to the Chinese World in San Francisco, the first and only Chinese/English daily in the United States, and the Humanity Weekly in Hong Kong. The philosophy of these papers were identical in their championship of democratic principles in government which coincided with my own beliefs.

Among all my objectives in life, there is one I feel particularly regretful about and that is that I was not effective nor influential enough to have a Confucian teaching institute established here to perpetuate his teachings. As a Chinese, I am profoundly tradition minded. As such, and with others of same mind, Confucius is always revered as a paragon of virtue and intellect. His teachings are the foundation to build families and even nations, and a source of our culture. I have always strived to be a good follower of his teachings.

(Center Front Row), 1947
Lai Shee and C.Q. Yee Hop's 16 children

Chapter 4

Who's who – 3 Family Generations

At my age, having just passed my eighty-first birthday, I have summarized briefly more than sixty years of my efforts, accomplishments, and achievements in business here. With me in Honolulu almost all of these years has been my family. My family has grown, and I am surrounded by numerous sons and daughters, large numbers of grandchildren and great-grandchildren. With respect to my early marriages, I had a few sad periods associated with them. Twice I became a widower. My first wife, Lee Shee died in 1902 and left me with four young children, three girls and a boy. My second wife, Chock Shee passed away in 1908 and left behind two little girls. My present wife, Lai Shee, is a kind, considerate, gentle, capable person. She shares my successes, happiness, and my life. She was a great help in raising the six children from my previous marriages. Together we have ten children (three boys and seven girls). We also lost two sons in one year, one in infancy and the other was almost five years old.

Altogether, I have four sons and twelve daughters. My eldest son, Yee Sing married Alice Lee. Their union provided me with two grandsons, Junion and Robert, and one granddaughter, Alsona. Hung Lum, my second son, married Elsie Tong, and they are parents to Cedric and Carolyn. The third son is Kwai Leong, who married Aileen Leong. Their children are sons Garwin and Carlson and a daughter Cherylene. My fourth son, Kwai Dick married Evelyn Lee and their infant son is Dennis.

Chun Quon (C.Q.)
and oldest son,
Yee Sing

My eldest daughter, Tai Moi, was married to Lee Akau, who is deceased. They have a family of four sons (one died at 18), Raymond, Gary, and William and four daughters, Amy, Eunice, Ah Kin, and Ah Sim. Yee Moi (number two daughter) is married to Leong Foon Yee, and they have two sons, Clarence and Albert, and four daughters, Frances, Doris, Velma, and Irene. Sam Moi (number three) married Wee Yee and they have two sons, Joseph and Walter, and one daughter, Nancy. Number four daughter, See Moi is married to Chang Say Chong. They have two sons, Bejamin and Clarence. Rosie Ng Moi (number five daughter) married Wing On Chong of Hilo and they have two sons, Ronald and Wendell, and two daughters, Roberta and Loretta. Clara Look Moi (number six daughter) is married to William Won of Berkeley, California. They have a daughter, Candace and a son, Peter. Number seven daughter, Helen Chut Moi is married to Lawrence Ting of Wailuku, Maui, and their sons are Kit Ming and Kit Hin and their daughters are Leslie (Ginger) and Laureleigh (Cookie). Patsy Bot Moi (number eight daughter) is married to Henry Hung Pui Chun. Their children are one boy, Roderick, and one girl Sandra. Anita Kau Moi, who is the ninth daughter, is married to Charles Luke. Number ten daughter, Vera Sup Moi, is married to Wilfred Lum. Carol Ann is their little girl. The two youngest girls are unmarried at this time. Betty Sup Yet number eleven daughter, is a student at the University of California at Berkeley and Doris Sup Yee, number twelve daughter, is attending the University of Hawaii.

All in all, at this time, my life is enriched with my sixteen children, twenty-two grandsons and nineteen granddaughters.

Along with my efforts to better myself during these many past years, I have endeavored to serve my community and my country to the best of my ability. My fondest hope is that I have succeeded in making some worthy contribution to posterity.

To those who so graciously honored me during my eighty-first birthday celebration, I convey my deepest appreviation.

Chun Quon's Family Group
1947
(3 generations)

COMMENTARY

According to an old Chinese legend "Wealth In A Family Will Not Go Beyond 3 Generations".

富不過三代

Coincidentally as a 3rd generation American Born Chinese (ABC), I am inclined to believe there may be some truth to this adage.

Following my grandfather's passing in 1954 (and several years after), there was a tremendous amount of tension and turmoil. Although the C.Q. Yee Hop Estate was administered by Hawaiian Trust Company and controlled by 5 appointed Trustees, a power struggle had nonetheless taken place among some family groups that lasted on-and-off for about 3 decades. Meanwhile countless millions were spent on court costs and attorney fees.

During this critical transition period, I had been living most of my adult life in California, so my knowledge and involvement in the family business was somewhat limited and obscured except for the occasional company board meetings which I attended as a director.

As a beneficiary and minor shareholder in the C.Q. Yee Hop Estate, my major concern was not so much about money or power, but rather to support whom I thought at the time would be the best fiduciary leader to carry on my late grandfather's legacy.

"Every kingdom divided against it will be ruined, and every city or <u>household divided against itself</u> <u>will not stand</u>".

(Matthew 12:25)

Thankfully about 25 years ago, the matter of succession was finally settled; however it appears questionable at this time to know whether or not the C.Q. Yee Hop's legacy will be able to carry on beyond 3 generations.

Another vital concern is regarding the preservation of old Chinese traditions. It seems the new "hip-hop" generation doesn't care much one way or another. They appear oblivious and much more interested in futuristic games and gadgets. On the other hand, being an eight-five year old traditionalist, I feel more strongly in favor of keeping our heritage alive as an ancestral obligation.

Traditionally, the Chun clan from Gong Bui Village in Guandong Province have proudly carried on for over 26 generations since the Sung Dynasty (960 -1279). Indeed this is an amazing accomplishment which, together with my late grandfather's legacy, should be righteously treasured and preserved.

"Make a contribution to the human race, leave a sweet fragrance for a thousand generations".
Chinese Proverb

造福人群流芳萬世

Although living to create an earthly legacy is commendable, a wiser use of time is to build an internal legacy into God's kingdom.

政民山檀前(側右翁壽在站)人夫其及禮啓孫長校學大夷威夏:分部一的寶貴(側左人夫陳在站)人夫明關嶽員議上山檀(側右人夫陳在站)特斯潘德長

Hawaii Territorial Governor, Mr. & Mrs. C.Q. Yee Hop and family Members with VIP Guests

海內外親友賀電

壽餅

CONGRATULATORY MESSAGES

頤性葆真
蔣中正
葦濤先生八旬晉一介壽

President, Chiang-kai Sheik
Republic of China

年高德劭
孫科敬祝
陳袞先生八十晉一大慶

Sun Ker, Son of Dr. Sun-Yet-Sen
Founder, Republic of China, 1911

善濤同志兄八十壽慶

渭水鷹揚未是奇 太平洋浪湧春思
記從壯歲倡行憲 看定全盤早下棋
議席名高徵福命 壽堂風暖望英姿
難忘努力開新報 壓倒香山萬卷詩

丁亥夏 伍憲子拜祝

陳袞先生八十晉一大慶

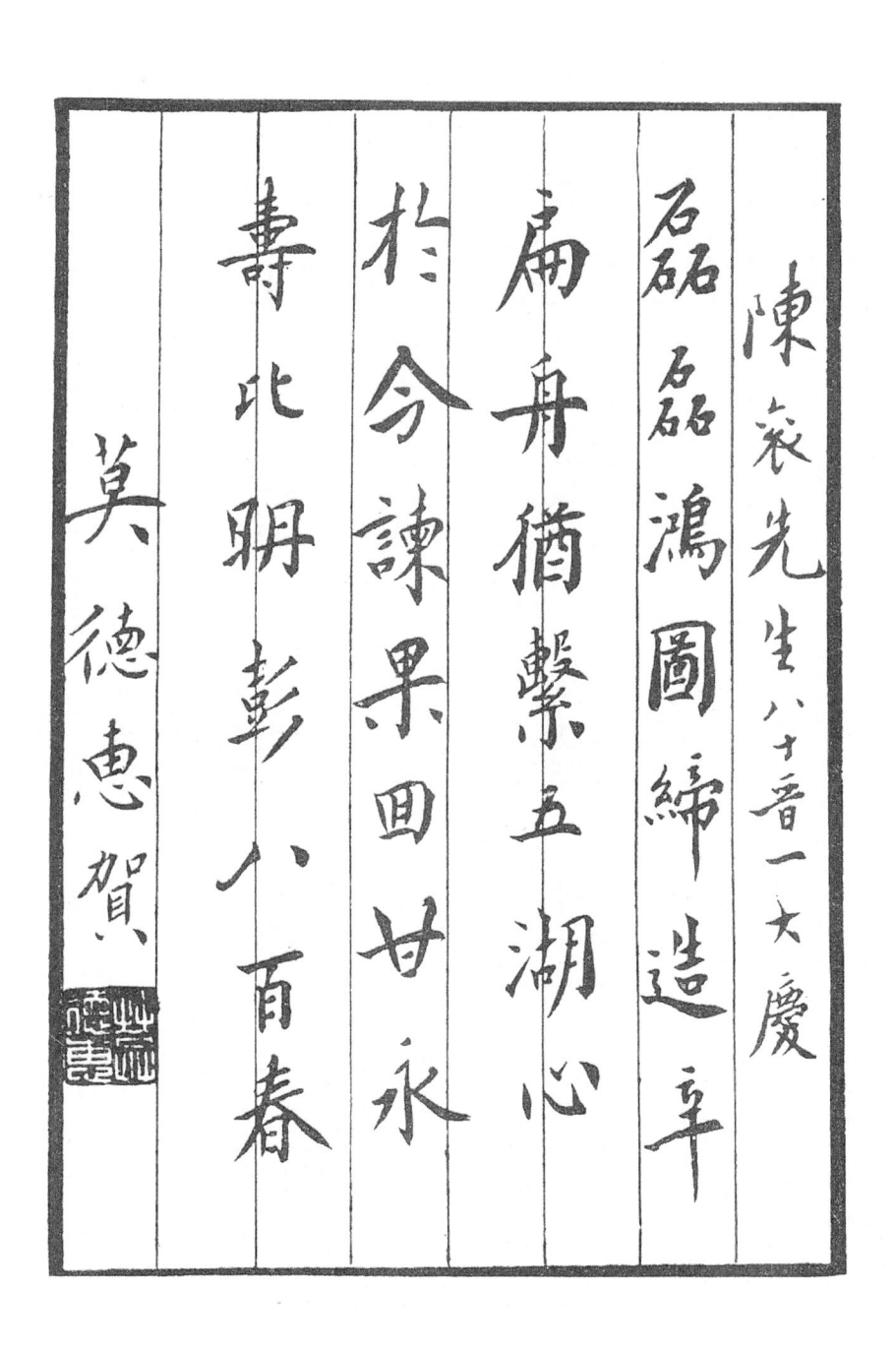

磊磊鴻圖締造辛
扁舟猶繫五湖心
於今諫果回甘永
壽比朋彭八百春

莫德惠賀

九五福曰壽
八千歲為春

善濤老先生八秩晉一榮慶

馮玉祥敬祝

如月之恆，如日之升，如南山之壽，不騫不崩，如松柏之茂，無不爾或承。

陳袞先生八十晉一壽　張羣敬祝

天保定爾 莫不興 如山如阜
如岡如陵 如川之方至 以莫不增

右書天保一章為
陳袞先生八十壽
王寵惠拜祝

陳家先生八十二大壽

眉壽無疆

宋子文敬祝

陳裏先生八袠晉一壽慶

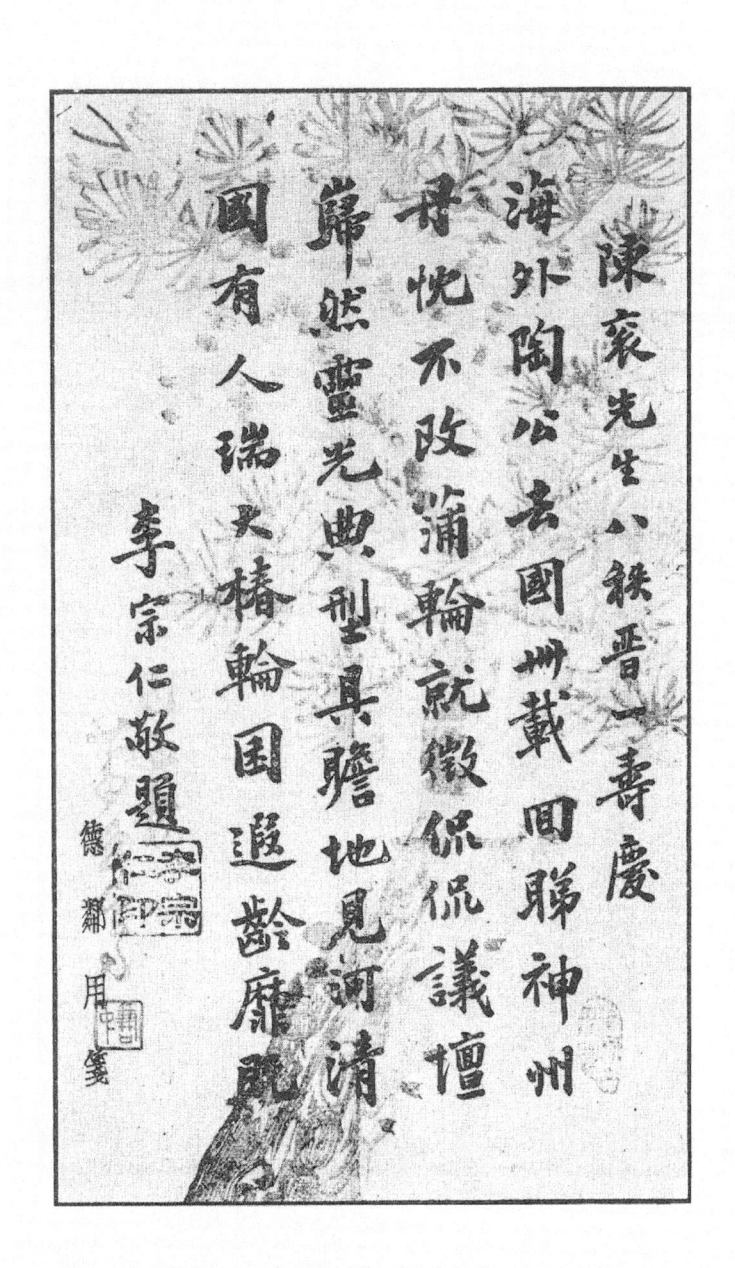

海外陶公去國卅載間關神州
丹忱不改蒲輪就徵侃侃議壇
歸然靈光典型具瞻地見河清
國有人瑞天椿輪囷遐齡康彊

李宗仁敬題

崔采騰輝

陳袞先生 八一榮慶

白崇禧題

陳袞先生八十一大壽

茂德高年

陳誠敬祝

陳褒先生八旬晉一大壽

箕疇五福一曰壽二曰富
蓬島上仙三千春八千秋

張厲生敬祝

碩德耆年

袁老先生八秩晉一榮慶

王世杰拜祝

敬子燕山呂義方階前玉樹煌煌行百年海屋春長在為賦同陵弄一觴賦賀

陳襄先生八十晉一大慶
梁寒操

陳袞先生八秩晉一大壽

介壽延開慶八旬　名高嶺表仰
完人　財輕篆籀惟行義術
擅陶朱　却尚仁樂育菁莪培
國本　咲看葉綵享天倫鴻麻
自備夢封頌不待陳詞祝大
椿

吳國楨拜譔

海外知交四十年
歸來無地看烽煙
如公福命天猶羨
東首傾杯入舞筵
微聞議席共稱尊
憲法完成感百端
無限壯懷今未老
祝君長壽保元元

善濤同志兄別四十年欣逢
今夏八十一歲壽辰今春又
浮槎手滬工賦此慶祝
　　　　　　　梁秋水

蠶歲勤勤〻稿棄儒因就商
萬里政多金祖國誓不忘
興學具慧眼巨資頻輸將
桃李滿天下育才即救亡半
生歷艱險寢息殊未遑慰
為壽之徵善乃被所藏玉樹
盈階前蘭枝繞膝傍卷耋
無違鑠尺理信有常烺然
祉華封福德隨無疆

陳袁先生六八秋晉一七壽
　　　　　　　王正廷敬祝

杖朝高壽趱旅程
去國卅年不厭生
裹法壺生甲溟席
民生考念苦鏖兵
聯欽比目魚山老
共戴千秋旨港航
直到珍頭无鈞健
長壽海國渡治平

某公南玉辰有作原
丁亥夏日照鈔
善濤老同志先八十一壽慶
盧敬安

天南隱逸此行似渭
水無綸又一年 樹木
樹人愁玉人游民游
坐度全荃漫嗟李泌
外傳薛鳳苟龍擺舞
傑覭航獻壽樂陶然

西波
陳袞先生八秩晉一大慶勉成俚
句卯春恭祝他尚希
王曉穎敬祝

李文樞先生之賀禮

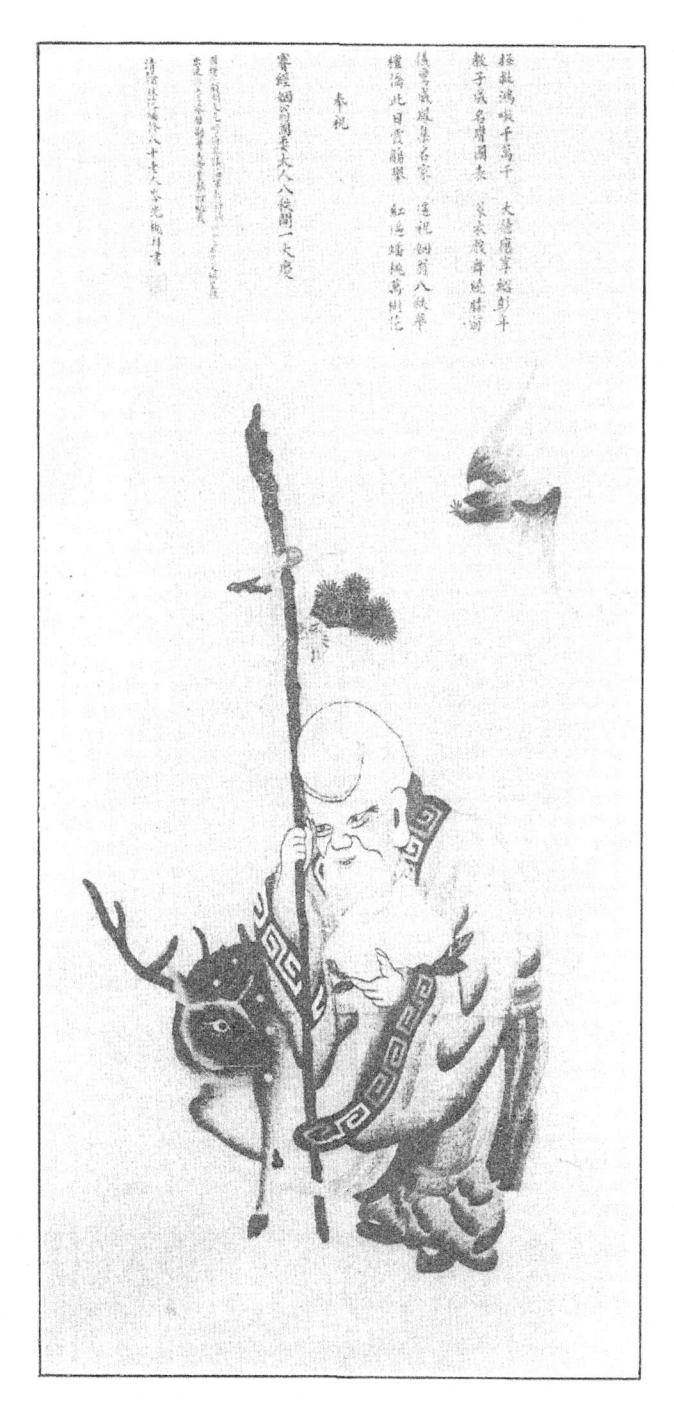

搖斾鴻嶪千萬千　大傷塵算紹彭斗
敎子成名曾圖泰　泉老彼群峨特別
後會冒歲嚴集名家　運視朝筯八紘華
壇海此日賞朋榮　虹海媼榧萬樹花

奉祝

寶繪綱紀蜀吳大人八袠開一大慶
因禮社之之
東

清溪社法眷弟八十老人谷光鎬甲書

Made in the USA
Middletown, DE
21 April 2022